Life Changing Learning for Children:
Resources That Work

by
Betty Hockett
and Grace Abbott

Robert A. Crandall, Ph. D., Executive Editor
Catherine Stonehouse, Ph. D., Managing Editor
Dorsey Brause, Ph. D., Consulting Editor

Light and Life Press
Winona Lake, Indiana 46590

ISBN 0-89367-020-0

Copyright © 1977 by
Light and Life Press

Printed in the United States of America by
Light and Life Press, Winona Lake, Indiana 46590

Explanation of C.E. Ministries Series
Training Texts

This book is part of the C.E. Ministries Series of the Free Methodist Church. It is one of twelve volumes which are a joint project of the denominational Department of Christian Education and the Free Methodist Publishing House.

These texts provide the basis for training persons ministering in Christian education at all age levels. The series is consistent with the church's organizational pattern and educational approaches. As you study these texts, you will be prepared to more effectively use Free Methodist curriculum materials and program guides within our denominational structure. Titles of the twelve volumes are:

I — Ministry to Persons:Organization and Administration

II — The Joy of Ministry: My Role in Christian Education

III — Ways and Means of Ministry: Focus on Christian Education

IV — Children as Learners

V — Youth as Learners

VI — Adults as Learners

VII — Life Changing Learning for Children: Resources That Work

VIII — Life Changing Learning for Youth: Resources That Work

IX — Life Changing Learning for Adults: Resources That Work

X — Expanded Ministry to Children: Program Guidelines

XI — Expanded Ministry to Youth: Program Guidelines

XII — Expanded Ministry to Adults: Program Guidelines

Certification for various positions of ministry in Christian education is achieved through study of the appropriate combinations of these texts. Note the requirements listed below for certifications in the Free Methodist Church.

Children's Ministries Leader
    Sunday School — Volumes I, II, III, IV, VII.
    Expanded Ministry/Midweek —
        Volumes I, II, III, IV, X

Youth Ministries Leader
    Sunday — Volumes I, II, III, V, VIII
    Expanded Ministry/Midweek —
        Volumes I, II, III, V, XI

Adult Ministries Leader
    Sunday School — Volumes I, II, III, VI, IX
    Expanded Ministry/Midweek —
        Volumes I, II, III, VI, XII

Director of Children's Ministries
    Volumes I, II, III, IV, VII, X

Director of Youth Ministries
    Volumes I, II, III, V, VIII, XI

Director of Adult Ministries
    Volumes I, II, II, VI, IX, XII

Director of Christian Education
    All twelve volumes

Contents

Introduction

Jim was a new and excited Christian. He would be great as a Sunday school teacher, we thought. He was also willing, and it wasn't long until he was handed a package of Sunday school curriculum and sent into a classroom to sink or swim as a teacher.

In a few months the director of Christian education discovered that although Jim could share his testimony with great excitement, he was totally frustrated when he tried to follow a lesson plan and do what was suggested in a teacher's manual. There are hundreds of Jims in many Sunday schools who have been handed a package of curriculum materials and, without any instructions on how to use them, have been expected to become effective Sunday school teachers. Many of them have become very effective. But whether we are using a saw, a violin, or Sunday school curriculum, we can use it best when we know how it was designed to be used.

Life-changing Learning for Children: Resources that Work has been written to help you know how to most effectively use your Aldersgate Graded Curriculum materials. It will be helpful for new teachers and probably will be a revealing review for those who have been teaching for some time. In the pages of this book you will discover what the writers and editors of the Aldersgate Graded Curriculum are trying to help you accomplish in each session. You will find tips for preparation and team planning.

About the Authors

Betty Hockett and Grace Abbott both write from a rich background of experience and current involvement in Christian education. They know what it is to be a Sunday school teacher of children and also have had experience as department or general leaders in the Sunday school. As mothers whose children are now teenagers or young adults they know intimately the needs and experiences of children. Both Grace and Betty have been deeply involved in curriculum planning and development and in the conducting of workshops to help teachers know how to more effectively fulfill the ministry that is theirs. Through these varied experiences they have been well prepared to write *Life-changing Learning for Children.*

The Use of This Text

Life-changing Learning for Children: Resources that Work has been designed for use by a group of teachers. The intent is that each person in the group will read the text at home and then meet to discuss the ideas which they have studied. Together the group will be involved in learning experiences which help to make the concepts of the book come alive and lead the learners in knowing how to use the ideas.

Interaction with others is an important part of learning. However, the text can be used by an individual if there is no class for that person to join. If you are going to be involved in an individual study, be sure to take the time to work through the "Can You?" "Would You?" and "It's Your Move" sections of each chapter. You could do some of the activities suggested in the *Leader's Guide* on your own.

It is our prayer that as you study this book you will grow in your effectiveness as a teacher.

Catherine Stonehouse
Director of Curriculum Ministries
Free Methodist Publishing House

Why AGC?

Can You
1. list five teaching methods Jesus used?
2. write out three good reasons for using Aldersgate Graded Curriculum materials to guide the study of a Sunday school class?

After studying chapter 1 you can.

During his third term on the mission field, suddenly and without warning, the young missionary was stricken with spinal meningitis. Miraculously God intervened, and now — several months later — completely recuperated, the missionary was speaking in his home church. He joyously recounted the events that led up to the miracle of healing. I wanted to listen, and I tried hard to focus my attention on my friend, the missionary speaker. This was my home church, too, and I remembered when this missionary was just a kid on the street. But my mind and my glance kept wandering across the church to a white-haired gentleman who sat near the front. For, when the missionary had been "a kid on the street" the white-haired gentleman had been a

9

concerned and active Sunday school leader. Week after week after week, he had knocked at the door of the home where a teenage boy — uninterested in church and rebellious — lived with his widowed mother and several brothers and sisters. The man's persistence matched the boy's rebellion. Some of us wondered why the man did not give up. Some of us asked him. He said, "Because the next time he might say yes."

Sure enough one day the boy did say yes and for the first time came to Sunday school. Later, the "kid on the street" — then preparing for his first term of missionary service publicly told his story. His father, hopelessly an alcoholic, had been in a hospital most of the time his children had been growing up. The family was poor, lived in a poor section of town, had few clothes, and bore most of the hardships that accompany poverty. When a man from the church began to call at their home to invite the teenage boy in whom he saw a great deal of potential to attend Sunday school, the boy resented him. He felt he did not need God or the church or this older friend. By his own admission, the only reason he gave an affirmative answer on the nineteenth week that his friend had come was to get rid of him. But the older man was not so easily shaken; he continued to come week after week, and for strange reasons which he could not understand, the boy continued to attend Sunday school. He met Christ, and his life was changed.

So, like an undercurrent in a fast-moving

stream, my thoughts raced as I listened to the thrilling account of God's miracle of healing. What if the man had given up? What if he had accepted no for an answer? What if he had felt the youth was not worth pursuing? What if he had given in to discouragement? What if he had listened to some of us who said, "Why do you keep going?" What if the church had failed to lead the boy to a life-changing relationship with Christ? What if he had not been helped to grow? What if? What if?

Today, the white-haired gentleman resides in a nursing home where with his radiant Christian testimony he continues to bless those who pass by. For twenty-two years he was a leader in the work of Christian education in his local church. He possessed the qualities and skills of leadership. He saw beyond the present to the potential.

Today that "kid on the street" is a director in the growing work of the mission organization he serves.

As teachers, we are given the privilege of working with God to lead boys and girls, young people and adults in life-changing learning. We, too, can have the thrill of seeing what God can do with the "kid on the street." We can rejoice in knowing that we had a part. Paul uses the analogy of the gardener to explain our part. God allows us to plant the seeds of His Word. Then follows the time of watering and tending the soil. Finally we see the harvest, a changed life, a young person serving God to the best of his or her potential.

The Master Teacher

But how can we teach so that lives will be changed? Jesus, the Master Teacher, provides our example. He was confronted with the task of teaching concepts and ideas. He had to break through traditionalism and legalism to reach the minds of the people. To do this He used simple but effective teaching tools.

Jesus taught in the idiom of His day with objects common to the culture — sheep, seeds and crops, a pool, fish, barley loaves. His story truths were based on the life experiences of His students. He made use of direct dialogue, object lessons, storytelling, questions, and occasionally, lecture. With simple illustrations which touched on the physical and emotional needs of His hearers, Jesus taught profound truths. Examine the parables: a candle under a bushel, new wine in old wineskins, a mustard seed, a lost sheep, a prodigal son, an unmerciful servant, the Good Samaritan.

When Jesus wanted to teach the truth of simple faith as a prerequisite to entering the kingdom of God, He used a child. Mark tells us that Jesus took the children up in His arms, put His hands on them, and blessed them as He said, "Truly, I say to you, whoever does not receive the kingdom of God like a child, shall not enter it" (Mark 10:5, RSV). In answer to the Sadducees' question about paying tribute to Caesar, Jesus asked for a penny. Then, using another good teaching tool, He asked a question, "Whose image and superscription hath it?" Listeners were involved in the lesson they were learning.

Another of Jesus' tools was His clear, straightforward manner of speech, always directed to the person at his own level of understanding and in terms with which he was familiar. "Give me to drink." "I am the bread of life." "I am the good shepherd." "I am the vine." "I am the light."

Another effective tool Jesus used was His own testimony: "I have spoken openly to the world; I have always taught in synagogues and in the temple . . ." (John 18:20, RSV).

Jesus *preached* to the masses, but most of His *teaching* was on an individual basis. He engaged Nicodemus in direct dialogue: Nicodemus came to Jesus, *"and said . . .*," "Jesus *answered and said . . .*," "Nicodemus *saith unto Him . . .*," "Jesus *answered and said . . .*," "Nicodemus *answered and said . . .*," "Jesus *answered and said . . . .*"

Of the Samaritan woman Jesus made a request: "Give me to drink." This request led into a life-changing dialogue. Step by step Jesus guided the woman to focus her thoughts on Him. He stimulated her curiosity: "I will give you living water." As Jesus continued the dialogue, the woman began to perceive that Jesus was not an ordinary man. By the time the disciples returned, she had discovered that Jesus was the Messiah.

13

Thus, Jesus accomplished His task of teaching. He did not begin by announcing the fact which He wanted her to learn. He involved her in discovering who He was. Because of His methods, His skills, and His genuine concern for people, the Master Teacher led those He taught to share in the life-changing discoveries.

Aldersgate Graded Curriculum materials have been designed to help teachers guide their students in life-changing discoveries. They can help you follow the example of the Master Teacher.

Let's look at some of the benefits available in the Aldersgate curriculum tools.

Benefits of AGC

As you teach in the Sunday school it is important to remember that the Bible is the textbook. Curriculum tools are designed to help teachers make the Bible live for boys and girls. Teach from your Bible but use your curriculum tools to guide you in helping the children discover what God has to say to them.

You will discover that Aldersgate Graded Curriculum materials recommend to you some of the same teaching methods Jesus used. Teachers' manuals suggest the use of direct dialogue, storytelling, object lessons, question approach, and getting the listener involved in interaction. Writers and planners of AGC have furnished many of these and other methods throughout the materials to help you facilitate change in the lives of your students.

Sunday school teachers are busy people. They do not have long hours to invest in the planning and creating of curriculum materials. Local churches are limited in the resources for producing curriculum. The teachers in a local church would not have the time or the resources to do from Sunday to Sunday what has been done for you by the producers of AGC. These materials are designed to help you, the teacher, involve students in meaningful learning experiences.

The teaching tools prepared for you by the Aldersgate associates are products of long hours of creative input, of planning, and of evaluating. Curriculum planners and writers from many parts of North America have contributed their best insights and ideas. Hundreds of Sunday school teachers across the continent have shared in the process of refining the curriculum tools. The results of their efforts are passed on to you, the teacher. The end results — Aldersgate Graded Curriculum resource packets and Aldersgate Graded Curriculum teacher manuals and student pieces — are not the product of one man's thinking or even of one denomination's thinking. They are the product of a group of people who think together and learn together — each giving and taking, each sharing ideas so that out of all this planning you have the best.

The kind of planning and care that goes into Aldersgate Graded Curriculum makes the finished product a launching pad for the creativity of teachers like you. Perhaps a launching pad is all you need. But maybe you feel that you are not bubbling over with creative ideas and need more help. Then AGC provides it. You will find the step-by-step procedure in Aldersgate Graded Curriculum easy to follow.

As in any curriculum material, there is always room for adaptation. The public school educator must build lesson plans from printed materials which have been produced to cover a wide spectrum of student use. It would be an impossible task for curriculum writers anywhere — either in secular or religious education — to prepare a curriculum which would meet the exact needs of every individual in every class in every church or school throughout the nation. However, this does not give credence to the philosophy that, "no one except the teacher knows these kids well enough to write curriculum for them." If that were true, think of the chaos that would exist in public schools across the land. Every teacher would decide on curriculum. There would be no orderly progression from one learning level to another. Aldersgate curriculum planners know the general characteristics of an age level and the basic operation of working with that age. A sound, solid curriculum has been developed from which adaptations may easily be made.

Aldersgate Graded Curriculum helps the teacher to meet the child, youth, or adult at his stage of development. Lay workers in the church are not expected to be experts in child or adolescent psychology. Yet knowing the special needs, abilities, and concerns of persons at different points in their development is important to effective teaching. Curriculum planners provide this knowledge. Topics, teaching methods, session plans, visuals, illustrations, and vocabulary in AGC have all been chosen with the students' development in mind. The teacher is helped to reach the students where they are.

Children are literal minded. Concepts must be presented as concretely as possible. Facts must not be distorted through the poor choice of words. Aldersgate writers help you avoid the use of symbolism or abstract terms as much as possible. For example, there is a children's chorus that talks about the devil being a sly old fox; it says, "If I could catch him, I'd put him in a box." Can you imagine the mental picture this brings to a child whose thought pattern is not mature enough for figures of speech? The devil must look like, and be the size of, a fox. If he could be caught and put into a box, surely he couldn't really be so bad or cause much damage. The song "The Devil Is a Sly Old Fox" is not used in AGC. The music chosen is within the comprehension of the children and is often directly related to the concepts the children are learning.

AGC is also structured to give a balance of ideas, insights, and information, so that no one aspect of learning is overemphasized while others may be overlooked. The teacher who uses no curriculum guide tends to plan week by week or a month at a time. Topics chosen often reflect the teacher's current interests or special concerns. A well-balanced study diet for healthy Christian growth may not be provided.

Aldersgate curriculum planners have asked, "What basic foundation of biblical concepts should a young person have laid by the time he or she graduates from the senior teen class of the Sunday school? What experiences are essential for Christian growth during the years of childhood and adolescence?" As these questions were answered the curriculum was built.

Any well-planned curriculum is designed as an interrelated package from nursery through the senior teen level. The total package is structured to provide the essentials for Christian growth and the laying of a firm foundation for faith. To gain the full benefit of the careful planning of the curriculum designers AGC should be used in all classes from nursery through senior teen.

Different "brands" of curriculum are not designed to complement each other. When individual classes within a Sunday school choose their own curriculum materials, problems arise. For example, in the brand X curriculum there is a young teen study on the book of John. Let's say the ninth grade teacher discovers this. John is one of his favorite books, so he uses brand X to give his students a study in John. Next year these students will be in the senior teen class. The Aldersgate senior teen materials provide a four-month study of the book of John. The students who used brand X will have had a double dose of John at the cost of not being able to explore some other important area of Scripture.

You are a Sunday school teacher in a denomination whose persuasion is basically evangelical. You are teaching in a denomination that has a holiness or Wesleyan-Arminian background. Your denomination has a particular message to share with the world. If you did not believe that your church's message was biblically sound you would join a different church. It is crucial that what is learned in the Sunday school is true to the doctrines of the church.

Most doctrinal or theological differences are based on varying interpretations of Scripture. These differences grow out of subtle variations of emphases, slightly different understandings of God, man, and their relationship to each other. The planners and writers of Aldersgate Graded Curriculum have been careful to present a Wesleyan-Arminian, holiness perspective. AGC is designed to introduce students to the exciting dynamic of our doctrine. No other graded curriculum materials are developed to do this. Members from each of the denominations in the Aldersgate association check the materials for you to be sure that they clearly and positively present the message of the church. Busy teachers such as you do not have to take valuable time to sift out hidden shades of meaning or interpretation that can come into conflict with doctrinal teachings of the denomination.

With all of this attention to creative tools for your teaching ministry, there is still a big job for *you* to do. All that goes into the AGC product is lost without you, the teacher, to give it a face and a voice and a loving concern. You alone can adapt the materials to fit the particular needs of individuals in your classroom. You alone can add the final refinements to present the materials at the level of understanding and comprehension which your students have reached. You alone, with the help of the Holy Spirit, can translate concepts and ideas from a printed page and help children, youth, or adults build them into their hearts and minds.

A Winning Combination

Competent tools for you, the teacher of children, are as necessary as a knife and fork at the dinner table. But there is more . . . much more. It is the teacher who is the warm body. It is you to whom the child responds. It is you he visualizes when he thinks about Sunday school. And when he sees you during the week, he smiles and says, "There's my teacher." He isn't thinking about the neat way you tell a story or about the simulation game you played at the beginning of last Sunday's class session. He isn't thinking about the special way you have of making biblical characters come alive for him. Your use of good tools in the classroom is something he is aware of, but he does not equate that with a happy time in Sunday school. His description of his Sunday school class would more than likely leave out all of the teaching techniques and curriculum materials you use, and concentrate on his impression of you as a person. So the best curriculum in the world will be effective only as it is translated through a warm, loving person.

The wise teacher will always remember that it is the teacher who sets the tone each Sunday, not the children. The teacher's reaction to the child largely determines the child's reaction to the session. Children are still on the childhood side of maturity, and they need emotional stability in a teacher. And they need love — warm, understanding, selfless love that flows easily and quickly to each child ... the pretty one, the vivacious one, the shy one, the slow learner, the troublemaker, the bright happy one, the listless, inattentive one ... God loves them all.

You are fortunate to be a Sunday school teacher. You are one of God's chosen. Of course there are times you feel inadequate for your job. Everyone who is conscientious and sensitive will have moments of feeling inadequate, whatever his job. But you are enrolled in this training course, and that is evidence that you want to do the best possible job you can. You are already aware that a teacher needs training. God has given you some innate skills which He will help you to develop through training and experience. Aldersgate Graded Curriculum brings to you the finest in tools. With this winning combination — training, skills, and tools — you can become what you want to be — the best possible teacher. God bless you.

Would You
1. list the teaching methods used by Jesus which you can also use?
2. explain why a teacher should use AGC?

Your Move
1. Talk to four or five persons of varying ages about Sunday school. What do they like about Sunday school? What don't they like? Try to discover what their comments indicate about the importance of the Sunday school teacher.
2. Check the inside front cover of an Aldersgate Graded Curriculum teacher's manual to find out what denominations are involved in the production of AGC.

What's Special About AGC ?

Can You
1. name the three components of a learning experience?
2. help children to begin building concepts?
3. outline the five steps to life-changing learning?
After studying chapter 2 you can.

The milk you drank today was most likely extracted from the cow through mechanical means. Very possibly it passed through a stainless steel milking machine into stainless steel and glass pipes, to a waiting stainless steel refrigerated truck, and into a mechanized processing plant. It came to you in sterilized containers, pasteurized, processed, and handled completely through automation.

But in the bygone days of rural America, the milk stool and the milk bucket were all the equipment Farmer Brown needed to perform that fascinating chore of milking the cow. The farmer's tender loving care and his milk stool and pail were his stock and trade.

23

The Sunday school teacher's three-legged stool represents something quite different from *that old milk stool,* yet uniquely similar to it.

The Threefold Objective

In every learning experience in life, three parts are present: knowing, feeling, doing. Farmer Brown *knew* that the cow had to be milked. But simply to know was not enough; he had to *feel* that he ought to get the milking done. Still to feel was not enough. Farmer Brown had to physically walk to the barn, take his three-legged milk stool from the nail on the wall, sit on it, and begin to make the streams of warm, white liquid flow into the milk pail. If Farmer Brown had stopped with *knowing* and *feeling* that he ought to go milk Old Boss, she never would have been milked. *Doing* was still needed.

For learning to take place a person must understand certain new ideas. That is *knowing.* He will respond in some way to those new understandings. That is *feeling.* Then he must act on that feeling. That is *doing.*

To further illustrate the threefold objective principle, let's say you want to learn to drive a car. You find an instructor who will teach adults, and you go for your first lesson. By sitting in the mock-up car, you learn the basics. Then one day you hear the instructor say, "Today we are going for a drive in the training car. You will drive." You understand the instructor clearly; you *know* the meaning of his words.

The instructor's words will evoke a response on your part. Either you will be eager to take your "maiden voyage," or you will be hesitant. But *you will respond* — positively or negatively; that is your *feeling* about what you know.

You get into the car, turn on the ignition, put the car in gear, release the brake, and move slowly forward, jerkily perhaps, but you move. Something is happening because you are acting upon the knowledge you have learned. And you are learning to drive a car by driving it — by *doing.*

As you continue to drive, you feel a new sense of accomplishment. Your new knowledge and your new feelings combined to allow you to do things you had not been able to do before.

New knowledge, positive attitudes, and opportunities to act on new insights are essential to life-changing learning. In the goal for each session the Aldersgate curriculum developers have set forth these three aspects of learning. The session is then developed with activities for discovering new knowledge, developing positive attitudes, and acting on learning. In your teacher's manual you have the ideas you need to lead your students in life-changing learning.

Concept Learning

Aldersgate Graded Curriculum is designed to encourage concept learning. *Memorization* may be accomplished by rote repetition, but *learning* takes place only when the student *wants* to learn.

It may be important to teach some hard, cold facts ... to ask the student to memorize simply through repetition ... at times. But if the learner is to discover for himself the joy of learning, and if he is to personalize the message you teach, he must build concepts instead of collecting unrelated facts.

Facts are the building blocks for concepts. How does the child build the concept that God is a God of love? The child learns the facts. God provided food for the Israelites in the wilderness. During the period of the judges He forgave them repeatedly. God forgave David's sins and sent the prophets to warn His people. Finally He sent Jesus to die for our sins. These are all *evidences* of God's love. As such, the facts are important. But they will be of lasting value to the child only as the teacher helps the child build them into his concept that God is love.

It is important to remember that children are building their own concepts. When you speak to your class, your words do not transplant the concept from your mind to the minds of your children. They take your words and illustrations, interpret them according to their experiences, and add them to their concept as *they* think the new ideas fit.

In an attempt to help preschoolers understand the concept that God is everywhere, one teacher ran into problems with the literal thought pattern of the very young. In her class was a bright three-year-old boy whose father drove a race car and whose whole family was racing oriented. Hoping to help little Darrell understand the concept, his teacher said, "You can talk to Jesus wherever you are because He is everywhere. You can even talk to Him when you are at the race track."

With almost no hesitation, Darrell said, "Nope. He wasn't there. I looked for Him in the bleachers, but He wasn't there. I went down to the pits with my dad, but He wasn't there either. I looked everywhere. He wasn't there."

This feedback was extremely valuable to the teacher. It allowed her to know what other facts Darrell needed to add to his concept of God as one who is everywhere. The wise teacher will listen carefully to students. Dialogue and response activities in Aldersgate session plans are designed to help teachers discover how children think and what is needed for the next step in concept building.

A Spiral Curriculum Design

A student in a Sunday school where AGC is used throughout will have the benefit of a carefully planned curriculum designed to help children build concepts. As the student matures physically and intellectually, the horizons of learning are widened. In the three-year cycle of each age level, primary through senior teen, the same twelve big ideas or concept areas are explored — one for each quarter. At each age level the child or teenager looks again at the big ideas. But each exploration of the big ideas is different from the others. Because of maturation the student has new needs and abilities. New ideas are discovered to be added to concepts. Progressively the big ideas are probed at a deeper level.

Because of this spiral design all of the essentials of the gospel are included for each age level. But the approach is varied and fresh at each level so that the study continues to be exciting and challenging for young people who use the curriculum throughout the complete cycle, nursery through senior teen.

The spiral curriculum design allows for a natural progression of an idea, from its simplest form for the youngest child, to its more complicated aspects for the mature adult. But it also allows for the planned repetition of an idea in order to fasten that idea — that concept — into the learner's mind until it becomes a part of his thought processes. As the learner progresses throughout the planned curriculum, the idea grows and is fostered and fed by the continuing spiral design which allows the learner to hear the story retold at his new learning level.

Home Involvement

The quarterly themes of AGC unify the study for children and young people throughout the Sunday school. Though they do not study the same scripture each Sunday during the quarter they study the same theme. This allows the family to share in discussing what is being learned in Sunday school. *Table Talk* is designed for parents to reinforce and to enrich the learning experiences of Sunday school. It is correlated with those quarterly themes. For example, when Sunday school curriculum dealt with Old Testament heroes, *Table Talk* guided the family in discussions on Old Testament heroes. Learning becomes a home-and-church-together experience through the use of *Table Talk.* The church and the home join forces to help children reach new levels of spiritual maturity as insights are gained from the family study.

Life-Changing Discovery Learning

Each session of Aldersgate Graded Curriculum is structured on five steps of discovery learning. These may not be set out as labels in each session, but they are present in the structure of the session, and a teacher can easily find them when preparing for a session. These five steps are:

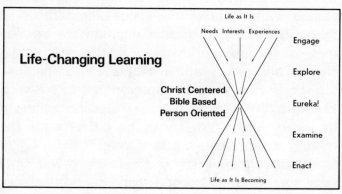

Engage. This is the attention grabber. The teacher arouses the student's curiosity. The student begins to think about things that will lead into the study of the morning. The first event of the class session should touch the interests or experiences of the children. Aldersgate Graded Curriculum provides help for you. Your teacher's manual suggests ways to engage the children's interest and bring their thoughts into focus on the session theme. A little practice will help you to skillfully lead the students from where they are into the next step in discovery learning.

Explore. The student's attention has been engaged, and you are ready to guide an exploration. You, the teacher, will guide the learning, allowing the student to make the discoveries himself. The student will be helped to explore scripture, ideas, and meanings to help him discover the truth of this session for himself. With younger children biblical facts are presented through Bible stories. The meaning of these facts will be explored as the children discuss the stories. With older children, questions are asked that will make the student dig into the session material for answers. Never frame questions that can be answered with a simple yes or no; use questions that require exploration for answers. Example: "Why did Jesus ask Peter three times if he loved Him?" "What was the difference in the three requests Jesus made of Peter?"

Young children enjoy exploration. Not until third grade and beyond can they effectively explore by working through the material on their own. But there are many other ways to help them explore the truth of the lesson. This can be accomplished through role playing; drawing what they conceive the Bible story to be about; telling the story back to the teacher with use of Nu-Vu figures, a bendable doll family, puppets, chenille-covered wire, or other such figures. In teaching young children, it is important for the teacher to remember that play is a child's way of learning. He needs to express himself and to gain new skills. He learns how to put information he has gained into use through play. The nursery teacher must provide creative playtime before and after the Bible story learning time, but the wise nursery teacher will also incorporate play throughout the session.

Eureka. You have arrived at the third step in life-changing learning. Eureka means "joy that comes from discovery" or "the light has dawned." The wheels are beginning to turn. From the exploration in step two, the student has made a fascinating discovery.

At this point the teacher is most dependent on the Holy Spirit. You cannot "program" a child to discover a truth at a given time or in a given way.

Because children vary in physical, emotional, intellectual, and spiritual maturity the light will come on at different times for different children. You cannot possibly predetermine the "moment of truth" for any child. But you can plan learning activities in which important discoveries can be made. You can pray that the Holy Spirit will lead the children to discovery. And often you can be aware of that moment when, through the help of the Holy Spirit, a child says, "Oh, I see!" He may not make a verbal statement. His discovery may be revealed to you through his body language or through his subsequent action(s). Just as you must depend on the Holy Spirit to bring enlightenment to the child, you must depend on Him to make you aware of the child's discovery. Very often with young children this will happen while they are *doing* an activity related to the session truth.

Examine. Now you have the opportunity to begin to help the student look at his own life in the light of what he has discovered. How will this truth affect his personal life? How will this truth affect him next week in his own world? This is the next step of discovery learning — *examine.* The teacher's job now is to help the student examine his own situation — his own personal life, his own personal sphere of operation in the world — in the light of the truth he has just discovered.

How do you help a young child examine his life and apply a new discovery? Many activities in the Aldersgate student manuals or activity books are designed with this purpose in mind. Class discussions and role play will also help children look at their lives. In some cases the teacher will need to work individually with a child at this point. Knowing the child and his home are necessary ingredients here.

For example, let's say that the teacher has helped the child to see that God loves us all, whether we are little, big, young, old, freckled, black, white, tired, grumpy, happy, or whatever. The child has discovered this truth. Now the teacher needs to help the child apply this personally. To six-year-old Susie, whose parents are divorced, the teacher may say, "God knows when you miss your daddy, and He cares when you feel bad. You can tell God what you think and how you feel. Have you done that?"

To nine-year-old Karen whose only sibling has recently been killed in a tragic accident you might say, "God loves you. He knows how you feel. When you think about your brother, does it help you to talk about him to God?"

To a child whose life has been untouched by personal pain you might say, "God loves you. He enjoys watching you play and be happy."

Enact. (Take action.) The last step in discovery learning and the most important one as it relates to the student's life is to *enact.*

A student sits in your classroom; you get his attention; he explores the lesson until he comes to the joy of discovery; then he examines the truth as it relates to his own life. But life-changing learning has not occurred until he goes out to act upon the new discovery. To challenge the student to act upon new insights is perhaps the teacher's greatest task. At this point also you can look to your Aldersgate teacher's manual for help.

Throughout chapter 2 we have discussed the "special" features of the Aldersgate Graded Curriculum. In summary, these are:

1. The Threefold Objective
2. Concept Learning
3. Spiral Curriculum Design
4. Home Involvement
5. Life-changing Discovery Learning

In each section of the chapter, the use of AGC with children has been only highlighted, because of space limitations. Your instructor will lead you through some activities that will assist you in making this material more personally yours, as you apply it to the responsibilities you have in your own Christian education program.

Would You
1. list the component parts of every learning experience?
2. describe briefly how you would help children begin to build concepts?
3. list the five steps to life-changing learning?

It's Your Move
1. Begin now to study ahead for each session you are responsible to present to the children. Chart the title and purpose, the responses desired, and the point at which you anticipate the five steps of life-changing learning will take place.

SAMPLE CHART

Date: Title:

As a result of this session what do I want my
students to

Know: _____

Feel: _____

Do: _____

What activities are planned to give the
children opportunity to learn the above

Knowledge: _____

Feelings: _____

Actions (doings): _____

What activities are planned for each step in
life-changing learning:

Engage: _____

Explore: _____

Eureka: _____

Examine: _____

Enact: _____

chapter

3 What's Available?

Can You
1. describe the purpose of each piece in the Aldersgate Graded Curriculum for use with children?
2. explain to parents what materials the Sunday school provides for them to use with their children in the home?

After studying chapter 3 you can.

Sunday school was over! No one had to tell the energetic fourth graders that it was time to go. As soon as they heard the first stirrings of others along the hall they gathered up their belongings and were out of the room in one grand swoop.

Marian sighed and muttered to herself. "I was sure the girls and boys would like this week's lesson, but I guess the only thing they look forward to in my class is the end."

"Morning, Marian," said cheerful Tom Arthur, the director of Christian education. "How did it go today?"

"Not so well," grumbled Marian sadly. "I can't

36

seem to get into things. I feel as though I'm just here at the head of the table trying to pour Bible facts into these kids. And as far as I can see, I'm not at all successful."

Tom stepped into Marian's room. "I'm sorry it hasn't been going well," he said gently. "I think, though, that you do have a point. Pouring facts in, as you say, isn't the way to genuine learning. At least not the kind of life-changing learning that we want. Of course, facts are important; we've got to have them. But children need to be guided into making some discoveries about what these facts mean in their everyday lives. We call it discovery learning."

"How I'd love to see my students make some life-changing discoveries!" responded Marian. "But how does it happen? How do I get them interested and excited about the Bible? How can I make Sunday school meaningful for them?"

Your name may be Jane, Margaret, Michael, or Dean, but could it be that Marian has expressed your feelings? Perhaps you feel as though you do all of the talking every Sunday, trying hard to pour facts into your children's minds. Or, you feel helpless in the face of the disinterest and boredom that is mirrored in the misbehavior of some class members. Would you welcome the opportunity of getting your students actively involved in the Sunday school session?

The Aldersgate Graded Curriculum has been designed to help teachers know how to lead their students in discovery learning. Week after week the materials provide varied suggestions for involving the children with the Scriptures in ways appropriate to their development and experiences. Activities are included to help children build biblical concepts and apply what is being learned to their everyday experiences.

But curriculum tools can help make learning more exciting and meaningful only if they are used. Understanding the materials and their purposes will make teacher preparation easier and possibly increase the effectiveness of the teacher. With this in mind let's take a look at the Aldersgate curriculum materials for use with children. Even teachers who have been using Aldersgate may be surprised by what they can learn from a fresh look at their curriculum tools.

The Teacher's Guide

Each Aldersgate teacher's manual is designed to help teachers and Sunday school department superintendents provide meaningful life-changing learning experiences for boys and girls. The manuals provide teacher enrichment, step-by-step plans for each Sunday, and instructions for using each of the other tools which make up the total Aldersgate Graded Curriculum package for a given age-group.

Teacher Enrichment

Each Aldersgate teacher's manual contains ongoing teacher training. Enrichment articles in the fronts of the *Nursery, Kindergarten,* and *Primary Teacher* give new insights about children and the teacher's responsibilities to them. Instructional articles may provide tips on storytelling, the use of puppets, or the importance of play in the young child's learning. Each week the *Junior Teacher* carries teaching tips in the session plans.

As teachers regularly read the section "Consider the Child," "Thinking of Your Children," or "The Lesson and Juniors," they will be gradually building a fuller understanding of the children with whom they work.

The *Kindergarten Teacher* carries a special feature entitled "Enrichment Ideas." This is a teachers' exchange. Teachers submit ideas which have worked well for them, and the ideas are printed for others to try.

Blessed is the teacher who is a growing person! For this reason the Aldersgate teachers' manuals provide materials for continuing education.

A Look at the Unit

Individual sessions of the Aldersgate Graded Curriculum are organized into units of study. Each session is separate but fits together with the others to form a unit. Instead of presenting isolated ideas each week, the teacher helps the children build ideas together into growing concepts. For example, in a unit entitled "I Am Growing" the kindergarten children discover that God has planned for them to grow in many ways.

On each of seven Sundays they consider different ways in which they are growing — in their abilities to choose, obey, take care of their bodies, share, get along with friends, and talk to God.

Chronology does not have meaning for young children. Study units for preschool and primary children are therefore organized according to conceptual themes rather than in chronological order. In the junior department the children are introduced to the chronology of the Bible. Fourth, fifth, and sixth graders will spend one year exploring God's plan as it unfolds in the Old Testament and another year studying the continual unfolding of that plan in the New Testament. The third year in their study is made up of units organized around a concept.

An introduction is provided for each unit of study. It gives the teacher a bird's-eye view of the unit. What purposes will the teacher plan to accomplish during the unit? What concepts will be explored? How do the ideas of the various sessions fit together to help the children build their concepts? These are questions which the unit introduction tries to answer. Unit projects are described, and items which need to be ordered in advance are listed.

The Weekly Session Plan

Aldersgate materials provide plans for the total Sunday school hour. The *Nursery, Kindergarten, Primary,* or *Junior Teacher* is the guidebook for the department superintendent or director as well as the Sunday school teacher's manual.

Assembly Time

With the weekly session plans the superintendent will find departmental worship ideas. These are designed to lead the children in a short, worthwhile worship time which relates to the purpose and theme of the Sunday school class session. Another important feature of the assembly time is the opportunity for the boys and girls to enjoy fellowship, sharing together in music and in prayer. Often the students can become involved in the worship presentations.

Church Time

For nursery, kindergarten, and primary children, the teacher's manual also contains plans for the church hour. This allows for a complete two-hour program which is all built around one central idea or purpose. The church hour is designed to complement the Sunday school hour. Young children learn new concepts by repeatedly working with them in different ways. During the Sunday school and church time the children will hear Bible and contemporary stories, sing songs, complete activity sheets, and possibly play games relating to the concept being explored that Sunday. When Sunday school and church experiences work toward a common purpose, the children are more likely to go home with one main concept well learned instead of having a jumble of ideas in their minds which may not have been understood and probably will not be remembered.

The Primary Church Time plans are designed to give the children experiences which will prepare them for participation in adult worship. A thirty-minute worship service is planned for each Sunday. It follows the pattern of an adult service, but each part is tailored to the primary child.

Be sure that department superintendents or directors and persons responsible for church hour activities have copies of the teacher's manual. Your Sunday morning ministry to boys and girls will be most beneficial if department superintendents, teachers, and church hour workers plan together for a coordinated program.

Teacher Preparation

When busy teachers begin their Sunday school preparation there is a temptation to skip over the first sections in the teacher's manual and go directly to the description of class time activities. That temptation should be squelched. Take time to travel through the session plan in a consecutive, orderly fashion. Be sure to stop and study the purpose or goal for the session. It has a very important function — it pinpoints the reason for the entire session. The detailed plans will fall into place more meaningfully when you have the session goal in mind.

Life-changing learning is made up of three inseparable parts — the facts one knows, the

42

feelings and attitudes one has toward those facts, and what one does to learn facts and feelings or what one does as a result of learning certain facts and feelings. In each session the teacher must be concerned about all three facets of learning — knowing, feeling, and doing. For this reason the session purpose has been stated in three steps:

1. The factual information the child should learn during the session,
2. The positive feelings and attitudes which we want to foster,
3. The behaviors which should be the expression of the learning of the new facts and attitudes.

With the session purpose in mind the teacher is ready to continue preparation. There are several parts to the preparation section. Helps and inspiration for the teacher, a guide for relating this session to the students, and a complete listing of materials and songs that need to be prepared are included. Good ideas often die very young because they were not planned early enough. Reading the Materials Checklist early in the week will help avoid the frustrations that come with late preparation.

"Class Time at a Glance" or "Lesson Preview," the boxed-in section at the beginning of each primary or junior session, gives a mini-view of what is to take place. After studying this overview the teacher will find it easier to understand the detailed class time plans.

Presession

Now it is time to think of the actual structure of the Sunday school hour. What does one do with the early birds? Aldersgate teachers' manuals provide suggestions for presession activities appropriate to the age-group. Through these activities the children begin the fun of learning as soon as they arrive at Sunday school. Interesting presession activities will go a long way toward preventing unhappy two-or-three-year-olds and bored older children. Most discipline problems don't have a chance to develop when children are busy and happy.

Each teacher may provide a presession activity in the classroom, or the presession activities may be set up in the department meeting room. The teachers in the department can then offer two or three activities from which all the children may choose. Teachers should take advantage of the presession time to visit with the children and learn about the events of the past week.

Presession activities are usually followed by the assembly time, which prepares the way for the class session. However, the assembly time may be scheduled at the end of the Sunday School hour as a climax to class time.

Class Time

Bible study and the application of Bible truths to life are the purposes of class time. For children the telling of a Bible story is the way in which biblical facts are introduced for exploration. But the teacher does not jump right into the Bible story as soon as the children enter the classroom. In each session ideas are offered to prepare the way for the Bible story. Conversation, discussion, illustrations, object lessons, or other activities are used to focus attention on the ideas which the Bible story will deal with. An important part of the young child's preparation is opportunity to move around and stretch some wiggly muscles before being asked to sit still and listen.

The Bible story is the focal point of the class session. The way in which these stories are told will influence whether the child thinks of the Bible as an interesting, exciting book or a dull book. Aldersgate teachers' manuals try to present the Bible stories in an interesting form. The story length and vocabulary vary at the different age levels to suit the needs of the children. Visual aids are also provided to help the Bible story come to life.

The time after the Bible story is also very important. A variety of methods are used for reviewing the story, finding out what the children think the story means, discovering how the biblical principles apply to their lives, and finding ways to do something about what has been learned.

Evaluate

While each session is still fresh in mind the teacher should spend a few moments reviewing it, evaluating what happened in the light of the session purpose. What evidence was there that the children learned what the teacher intended them to learn? What progress did the children show? What needs were obvious? The *Kindergarten Teacher* provides a special section, "Looking Back," to help teachers with their evaluation.

Music

Music is written into the Aldersgate materials because it is an important teaching technique. Music can be used to give directions to young children and to help them move on to a different activity. Action songs allow for much needed movement. Concepts set to music will sing through the child's mind during the week. The songs chosen for use in the curriculum materials carry the concepts being taught through the Bible stories and other learning activities. They have words which the children can understand and tunes which they can learn. Many of the songs will be new to the teachers. But as teachers learn two or three new songs each quarter they will gradually build a new repertoire of music which teaches important concepts.

Memorization

Scripture memorization has traditionally been a part of Sunday school. The planners of the Aldersgate materials have carefully chosen verses for memorization which have meaning for the children. They contain concepts which are valuable to have in mind for life. Much of the memorization program for juniors is made up of passages of Scripture rather than isolated verses.

If Scripture memorization is to be of value to the child, the verses and passages memorized must be understood. The teacher's manual contains ideas for helping the children grasp the meanings of the verses. Games are provided for making memorization fun, and opportunities are given for using memory passages as choral readings in the worship time.

Adaptations

The Aldersgate teachers' manuals provide the teachers with helps for adapting session plans to meet the needs of older or younger children within the department. The *Nursery Teacher* includes a separate section for teachers of two-year-olds. In this section the teacher will find simplified stories and instructions for using selected activities from the session plans for threes. In both the *Primary* and *Junior Teacher* varied activities are provided for the younger and older children.

Teaching Resources

Adequate visual aids greatly enhance the effectiveness of any teaching. The Aldersgate Graded Curriculum provides quarterly packets of attractive, usable visuals. Session plans are written with the assumption that each teacher has the resource packet available for use. Colorful flat pictures, Nu-Vu figures, puppets, diagrams, murals, games, posters, and bulletin board ideas are only some of the items which may be found in the resource packet. Visuals are used to illustrate the Bible story, to let the children express what they have been learning, or to help in applying biblical concepts to life. Many of the resource items can be used and manipulated by the children. This allows for the children to become actively involved in learning.

Student Manuals

Student manuals are designed to involve children in the learning process. Activities in the Aldersgate student manuals have one of two general purposes: (1) to lead the child in an interesting review of the Bible story or passage; (2) to help the child make real-life applications of Bible teaching.

The student books for nursery, kindergarten, and young primary children are in the form of activity sheets. These pages provide necessary activity for young children who still have so many muscles to wiggle with but so few to sit still with. But they do more. Each Sunday, after the sheet has been completed, give ample opportunity for the children to use what they have made. The teacher can talk with them while they manipulate the item, helping them further understand the Bible story or the life application. Sometimes the teacher can use the activity sheet as a visual aid while the Bible story is told.

Older primaries and junior boys and girls are

provided with personal study books. *Learn and Do* is the workbook for older primaries. Puzzles, riddles, matching statements, complete-the-story, thought questions, and Bible verse reviews are all in *Learn and Do* to help the children review the Bible facts and as an aid in discovering the meaning of the Scriptures for their lives. Bible study aids, review games, puzzles, skits, pictures, and thought questions are some of the smorgasbord of activities offered in *Explorer I* and *Explorer II* for juniors.

Primary and junior teachers each have two student books to choose from. *Primary Activity Time* is designed for younger primaries who are just developing their reading and writing skills. *Learn and Do* is for the second or third graders who are anxious to use their newly acquired skills of reading and writing. *Explorer I* is a simplified version of *Explorer II.* It features larger type with fewer and easier things to do. *Explorer II* often includes extra activities for the faster juniors.

Grade designation has been left off the primary and junior student books. This has been done so that the teacher can use the book which best suits the need of his or her class. Some third graders may be most comfortable with *Activity Time.* A first grade class may be ready for *Learn and Do* halfway through the year. A fifth grade teacher may find that although her class last year enjoyed *Explorer II,* this year's class works best with *Explorer I.*

Working with the Home

Effective Christian education calls for the church and the home to work together. The Aldersgate Graded Curriculum provides parents with many helpful tools.

Table Talk is a daily devotional guide correlated with the Sunday school materials. For each day there is a scripture passage, an illustration, and discussion questions which tie in with the theme of the primary and junior Sunday school sessions. Each week reference is made to what the preschoolers have been studying.

Curriculum-related Bible storybooks and weekly story papers also help bring the home and Sunday school closer together. The nursery and kindergarten Bible storybooks and the primary story paper, *Primary Friend,* all include the Bible story told in Sunday School. Parents can continue to review and discuss the story with the child and thus strengthen the effectiveness of the Sunday school.

Listen, Primary Friend, and *Discovery* are weekly papers containing contemporary stories, poems, and enjoyable activities for the children. Parents will become involved in reading the stories to younger children. In some issues of *Listen* the parent will find helpful tips for relating to young children.

Activity sheets can also have an influence in the home. Sometimes they are designed for use at home. Often the child is instructed to tell the

Bible story using the activity sheet.

If parents are to use curriculum tools effectively they need to know how the various items are designed to be used by them. Informing parents about the materials that are coming into the home and encouraging them to extend the ministry of the Sunday school by using the tools is an important responsibility for the Sunday school teacher and department staff.

Would You
1. describe the purpose of each Aldersgate Graded Curriculum piece designed for use with the age-group you teach?
2. explain how Aldersgate Graded Curriculum items might be used in the home?

Your Move
1. Look through the student manual designed for your class. Note the variety of activities. How many activities are designed to review or explore the Bible story? How many deal with life applications?
2. As you prepare your Sunday school lesson this week, reread the unit introduction. Also be sure to read the materials designed to help you prepare.
3. Plan to try a new idea suggested in your teacher's manual.

4 Be Prepared

Can You
1. list four activities that should be part of the teacher's pre-quarter planning?
2. explain why it is important to begin Sunday school session preparation early in the week?
After studying chapter 4 you can.

Judy sat with an open teacher's manual before her. It was late Saturday night, and she was looking at the material for the first time. "But I was so busy," she rationalized. "This is the best I can do for preparing my Sunday school lesson. Next week I'll do better."

You are probably a very busy person with home responsibilities, possibly a heavy work load at your place of employment, and other church obligations in addition to Sunday school teaching. There will be all sorts of reasons for postponing your lesson preparations.

Sunday school teaching requires self-discipline. This involves being disciplined enough to maintain good, regular study habits.

Prequarter Preparation
Individual Preparation

The very best time to begin your personal preparation for the new quarter is right after you receive your new materials. Look everything over thoroughly. Take out each piece in the *Teaching Resources* packet to get an idea of what is ahead. Read the unit introductions and make notes about materials you will need to collect or prepare. Note the Bible stories and the objectives for each session. See how the units fit together. This helps you to have an overview which will make each session more meaningful.

In the unit introduction you may find projects that take advanced planning. Perhaps there will be some activity which you need to publicize or communicate with parents about. Make note of this, planning the dates when publicity and communications should be sent out. Decide on dates for class or departmental parties or service projects. Field trips should be thought of and planned in advance also.

Make note of new songs. Decide to learn at least one new song each quarter — or even better, one a unit. This way you can soon develop a good repertoire.

Visualizing a new song is the ideal way to quickly teach it to nursery or kindergarten children. Find simple pictures that depict the words. Mount them on bright paper and use as flash cards or a flip chart. Primaries, especially the younger ones, can benefit from having a new song visualized also. Older primaries and juniors profit by seeing the words printed on a large chart or on a chalkboard.

As a teacher, you are a model! Pupils are looking to you as an example. This calls for you to be a pacesetter in learning Scripture passages and verses. You can be assured of personal spiritual benefits as you learn not only the short, easy verses but also the longer, more difficult passages.

Aldersgate editors have done all that they can to make the visuals in the resource packets as usable as possible with a minimum amount of work required from you. However, there are often items that need to be cut out and prepared ahead of the Sunday morning sessions. As you take this initial look at the packet, you will see which pieces need beforehand preparation. It is helpful to cut out all of the Nu-Vu story figures before the quarter begins. Inexpensive manila envelopes or small, flat sacks provide good storage places for the figures. Label each container with the story title, date to be used, and the diagram of how the figures are to be placed.

"One more thing to do," said Wayne, groaning. "I don't have time to cut out paper dolls. Guess I won't use the visuals the Sundays we have Nu-Vu. It's just too much bother." Have you ever felt that way? Why not enlist some help?

If you teach juniors, plan a meal or a party for

the class. While they are waiting for the eats have them cut out the items in the resource packet. As teacher and students have fun together in an informal setting, rapport will be building, and your Nu-Vu figures will be cut out. Actually, you will have killed two birds with one party!

Another source of aid could come from the high school department. The wife of a male teacher could be enlisted to assist with this part of his responsibility. The teacher's capable children might be asked to help with preparation of the visuals. There may be an older woman in your church who still is anxious to be involved in some way, though she is not able to teach. Such a person might also appreciate being asked to be a prayer partner for you and your class.

Department Preparation

Having the department leader and teachers meet together is an important way of beginning each quarter. Teachers' meetings *can* be exciting and meaningful. They can be a lifeline of strength and encouragement, doing a great deal toward fostering good morale which is necessary to Sunday school health and growth.

The ideal time for meeting together is about two weeks before the beginning of the quarter when the new curriculum materials are in hand. Praying over common concerns and interests should be a priority for the time you are together. Then go through the curriculum pieces together and share your ideas with each other. Scan session titles and goals to discover the flow of the unit. Read the unit introduction together. Here are some things to think about at your next departmental teachers' meeting:

1. What shall we do to improve the appearance of our classroom or departmental room?
2. Which of the unit activities would be most meaningful?
3. What special items do we need to collect and prepare?
4. Can we divide some of the nitty-gritty responsibilities? (One person doing the room decorating, others preparing different presession activities.)
5. Look at the session titles. Think about them in relationship to your life as an adult. What can these sessions mean to you?

Spend time in praying together and in sharing both joys and concerns about your teaching.

If your Sunday school is small, with only one teacher for each age level, you can still meet together. Even if it is not practical for you to have a group curriculum study, it will be beneficial for you to pray together and to have a renewed sense of teamwork.

Weekly Preparation

Now that you have the unit preparations completed, it's time to begin the actual session preparations. What is your weekly study schedule?

Meet Jerri. She teaches the five-year-olds. Late one Saturday night when she finally got around to opening her teacher's manual, she had a super idea! "I'll have the kids make little gifts to give to the grandmothers' class. This will go along just perfectly with our unit on sharing our love for God with others." She excitedly began to plan. "Let's see, we'll need some aluminum foil. Yes, I have that. Then we'll have to have plastic flowers and some moss. . . ." Her enthusiasm suddenly faded. That great idea died right then and there. If only she had planned earlier in the week, the idea could have become a good project.

Let's look at a preparation schedule which will lead to effective teaching.

A Preparation Schedule

Sunday afternoon or Monday: While you can still remember it clearly, evaluate the session just completed. Record your observations of student responses. Then, spend thirty to forty-five minutes with the next session. Read the items at the very first of the session, taking special note of the goal. Think how this session fits in with the unit. Check to be sure that you nave in mind the special items you will need to secure or prepare.

Read through the whole session chronologically and thoroughly. Then during the week as you mow the lawn, paint the garage, clean out the basement, vacuum, or drive back and forth to the office, you can think about the session, looking for appropriate life illustrations and how the concepts can speak to the needs of your students.

Be sure to read the Bible story, even if it is a very familiar one. Remember, there is always something new in each reading of the Scriptures. Begin now to memorize the Bible verse that is to be emphasized and remembered.

Tuesday and Wednesday: Review the Bible verse you memorized. Pray about the lesson. Pray for your pupils individually. Ask God to help you know how this session should be individualized to meet their particular needs and situations. Continue to watch for real-life illustrations.

Wednesday or Thursday: Thoroughly prepare the entire session. Make a written session plan as a reminder of how you will proceed on Sunday morning.

Prepare the sample activity sheet or workbook page.

Be certain that the items from the resource packet are prepared.

Practice telling the Bible story, using the visuals.

Prepare any auxiliary aids (word cards, puppets, or charts).

Check to be sure every needed item is on hand, either at home or in the classroom. If you need audiovisual equipment find out for sure that it will be available and ready.

Friday: Review the memory verse. Continue praying; be sure to pray for the other teachers and leaders in your Sunday school.

Saturday: Put the finishing touches on the lesson. Have everything that you are going to take gathered together in one place so you have no worries on Sunday morning.

This preparation plan may not fit your needs exactly. Adapt it. But remember these four things as you plan your personal preparation schedule:

1. Read through the entire session plan early in the week.
2. Pray each day for your students and the next class session.
3. Plan the session thoroughly before Saturday night.
4. Take a few minutes Saturday evening to put the final touches on your preparation.

Actually, preparation is complete only when a teacher is well acquainted with the children in his or her class. Really knowing them involves spending time with them other than during the Sunday school hour. Visiting in their homes, having them in yours, going to events the children are involved in (games, recitals, school events), socializing, and having fun together are important. It all helps to make the time together in class more meaningful. Also, each time you are with the boys and girls you have new opportunities for demonstrating your love for them. It is the evidence of your love for them that will make the most difference in their classroom response and behavior.

Adapting Curriculum

Curriculum should be a springboard for your own creative ideas. Aldersgate writers and editors know that they cannot produce sessions that will satisfy every teacher and every student in every situation all of the time. They expect you to adapt each session to meet the needs of your boys and girls. Familiarity with the curriculum and knowledge of your children, combined with experience, prepare you to adapt session plans wisely.

Most Sunday school sessions are not long enough to use all of the suggestions in the teachers' manuals or all the items in the student book. There is no law that says you must "get through all the material." In the light of your students' needs, choose the most important learning activities. The teacher may have to do part of the work on the activity sheet before class so that the children will be able to complete it. Be sure to plan the use of available time so that you can bring the session to a satisfying conclusion.

Children vary in their abilities, and this may call for adaptations in materials. Slower children will need more help to complete activities and may not have time for everything that is provided. If an activity sheet is too easy, it could be made more fun for a preschooler by providing touch-and-feel items to be added (buttons, fabric, rickrack, lace, yarn, sandpaper, or straw). The activity sheet could be mounted on a construction paper background. When primary or junior manuals are not challenging enough, supplement them with other projects. Ideas for such projects are often found in your teacher's manual.

A Personal Session Plan

To write a session plan or not to write a session plan — that does seem to be the question with many teachers. "But isn't a session plan what is in my teacher's manual?" you ask. The answer is yes. However, you still need your own specific plan of attack. Mental notes are fine, but unfortunately they sometimes become fuzzy in the press of Sunday morning activity. It is wise to write down your plan so that you will have no doubt as to where you are going and how you are going to get there.

An outline for a written session plan might look like this:

My goal for this session,

Scripture verse to be emphasized or memorized,

Songs or finger plays (preschool),

Visuals needed,

Presession activities,

Attention getter,

Bible story (in outline form),

Activities (possible questions and ideas for conversation),

Alternates,

Closing.

On your session plan, check the items that could be left out if time becomes a problem. You can also add items that can stretch the session if necessary.

Your session plan can be made to fit into your Bible so that the Bible is the focal point of attention during the class time. Once the plan is written, it usually turns out that you need it less; it is a part of you.

Would You
1. list four activities that should be part of the teacher's pre-quarter planning?
2. explain why it is important to begin Sunday school session preparation early in the week?

Your Move
1. With the other teachers and leaders in your department (or total Sunday school) plan a time when you can get together for a planning session similar to the one described in this chapter.
2. Make your personal preparation schedule and follow it this week.
3. Write out your own session plan for next Sunday. Put it in your Bible and teach from it on Sunday morning.

On Sunday Morning

Can You
1. give three reasons for having presession activities at Sunday school?
2. match Aldersgate Graded Curriculum pieces with the correct age or grade group?

After studying chapter 5 you can.

It was Sunday morning. Marian parked her car and walked into the church. It was early yet, and most of the pupils had not begun to arrive. As she walked past the primary assembly room, Marian noticed that Jenny, the primary director, was busy adding the last touches to an interesting display of seashells with two bright starfish alongside. She hurried on towards her room, passing the kindergarten room just as Jon, the college student who was helping with the fours and fives, turned on the record player. "Hi, Jon," she said quickly. "That music sounds nice." She noticed that the paper and crayons were all out on the table ready for the earlycomers' presession activity.

Just as Tom Arthur, the director of Christian

education, rounded the corner at the other end of the hall, Marian heard a two-year-old voice beginning to rise mournfully. "Good morning, Tom. Sounds as if Timmy Jenkins is here early again. Bless his heart, he still isn't quite used to this business of Sunday school."

Tom smiled. "Fortunately, Mrs. Benton is always here early with books or pictures or maybe a puzzle to take Timmy's attention. By the time his big sister gets him hauled all the way into the room he usually forgets his tears and is ready for action. Am I thankful for teachers like Mrs. Benton and you, who are here in plenty of time to get ready for these unexpected — or even expected — emergencies! How did things go for you this week, Marian?"

Marian put her books down on her classroom table. She was glad for the chance to share what God had done. "This has been a great week. Our Bible story for today is such a familiar one that I was tempted not even to reread it. But I decided to do just as we had talked about in our training session, so I dutifully read it. You know what? God really spoke to me and showed me some new things in there. It was great! Then next, I decided to learn the memory passage. It's kind of a hard one, and memory work isn't my cup of tea anymore, but it was amazing! God gave me some new insights into himself as He helped me learn those verses."

Tom looked more pleased than ever. "Sounds as though you did have a profitable study time.

But what about a written session plan? As I recall, you weren't sure that was necessary."

"Right here it is," answered Marian, opening her Bible to reveal her notes. "I didn't think I'd go that far in preparation, but I did. Funny thing, writing it out wasn't hard at all. I also came over here after work on Friday and got my room all fixed up. Having everything done ahead really does eliminate that old feeling of frustration that I always seemed to have on Sunday mornings."

Tom seemed really impressed as Marian finished. "That's great, Marian. I gather that you've discovered Sunday school preparation can be exciting. I'll try to get around after class and see how your session went. Right now I'd better get on down the hall. I want to thank Anna Moore for preparing all of the visuals for the nursery department. That was certainly a help to Mrs. Benton and her teachers."

The Sunday School in Action

It's time for Sunday school to begin! And what time is that? The moment the first pupil arrives — that's the beginning of Sunday school.

Presession

To be ready when the first child arrives you will need to be early. Set up at least one, but preferably two or three, of the presession learning centers suggested in your teacher's manual. At the centers you might have review or memory work games from the resource packet.

Creative projects, puzzles, or music activities might be offered. The purpose of these pre-session activities will be to help in review or to set the stage for what is going to happen during the morning. These presession activities can be done departmentally or by individual classes.

This is also an excellent time to enlist the children to help in decorating the room. Remember, the appearance of your room is important. Keep it neat. Change the bulletin board displays and decorations regularly. Plan to let the children share in making their room an attractive place. Even twos and threes can help by placing a picture or cutout on a bulletin board. Some fours and fives can help with simple cutting; all of them can help to arrange a bulletin board. Primaries and juniors are capable of helping to plan room decorations as well as to make them. Everyone is having the fun of working together to make the room attractive, using things that go along with the current unit or season, while the wise teacher initiates conversation that is contributing to the atmosphere for learning.

These early minutes are also the perfect time for children to share their news. Teacher can notice the new shoes or new shirt or tooth that is missing, or listen to the story of the six new kittens. Listening and noticing are part of loving!

Presession activities can end at any time that you see interest is waning. You may choose, if pupils are happily busy, to allow them to continue for a few extra minutes. Of course this would happen only if you are not meeting for worship with others. You would not want to infringe on time that someone else had planned.

Worship Time

The smoothness of transition from presession to the worship time can be aided by having a signal which is known to teachers and students. Nursery teachers may begin to sing "Let's Pick Up Toys." As they sing, they join the children in putting away the materials they have been using. In the kindergarten, primary, or junior department the pianist may begin to play. This lets the children know it is time to put materials away and to join others in the assembly area. Provide three to five minutes for transition.

Worship time, planned and led by the department superintendent or director, should not exceed fifteen or twenty minutes, one fourth of the total Sunday school time. Music, announcements, recognizing birthdays and visitors, and a presentation that goes along with the theme of the session can all be included. Remember, Aldersgate teachers' manuals contain ideas for this part of the session. Children can also profit by sharing prayer requests followed by a time of group praying. Worship time will be most meaningful for children when it is conducted separately from that of the youth and adults.

A closing rather than opening worship — not both — could have advantages for primaries and juniors. Being together at the end of the session allows opportunity for the department leader to tie together the whole morning. It also provides a chance for the classes to share something that they did during the session while it is still fresh in their minds.

Many churches have only one assembly time in which all children are included. "How can I use the department worship ideas in the teacher's manual when I have all the children to work with?" you may ask. That is a good question.

First, plan with the nursery teacher and the kindergarten teacher for their children to spend the entire Sunday school period in their own classrooms. A team of two teachers in each preschool class can lead the children in pre-session activities, which may continue into the first few minutes of the scheduled Sunday school time. The voices of preschoolers will not disturb others as they have a time of singing together in their classroom. By meeting separately for the entire hour the preschoolers will have more time to act out their Bible stories and become involved in other enjoyable learning activities.

The primaries and juniors will then meet together for the worship time. If you are in charge of this group, be sure to have both a primary and a junior teacher's manual. Study the manuals and find things in common that can be used in the worship. Songs and seasonal emphases can tie the group together. Sometimes use the worship feature ideas from one teacher's manual, some-times from the other. Ask God to help you lead the children in real worship.

Class Time

John Cook and his noisy, energetic third graders hurried into their classroom. The boys and girls found their places at the table as John immediately showed a teaching picture that was covered with squares of bright paper. "Under these squares," he explained, "is a Bible picture that you have seen before. On these slips of paper that I'll give you are questions. As you answer your question you can lift one square from off the picture. Let's see how quickly we can discover what the picture is about." The children were soon happily involved in this game (actual activity from a fall *Primary Teacher*). As soon as the picture was discovered John went right on to tell the new Bible story as everyone listened eagerly.

John's actions indicate that he has accepted his students as they are. He knows that they are energetic and will channel their energies toward whatever grabs their interest — trying to make the little girl on the next chair squirm, or preparing for a Bible story. John also knows that third graders are curious and enjoy a game. Before they have a chance to begin some undesirable behavior, John uses a game to *engage* their minds and begin to lead them toward involvement in exploring the Bible. Aldersgate teachers' manuals provide a variety of activities to meet the children where they are, to engage their minds, and to draw them into learning.

The time for *exploring* the Bible should be the priority item on the session schedule. Tell the Bible story in such a way that the boys and girls will be fascinated by God's Word. If older juniors begin to lose interest in listening to Bible stories, let them take turns telling the stories. They will enjoy using puppets with the stories or preparing recorded radio dramas of the biblical events. As you involve children in Scripture study activities, they are learning attitudes toward the Bible. Be sure that those attitudes are positive.

After the teacher and children have together explored the Bible truth, they can begin to *examine* what it means to them personally. *Nursery Activities, Kindergarten Activities, Primary Activities, Learn and Do,* and both *Junior Explorer I* and *II* are designed to help in accomplishing this important step in discovery learning. Your teacher's manual may give other ways of making the life application. Even when time is limited, be sure to include some type of activity which will help the children examine the relevance of the Bible truth to their own lives.

Tim listened intently as Marilyn and Troy told of miracles God had done in the lives of people they knew. "That's neat," broke in Tim. "I didn't really believe these things we've been learning in Sunday school. But if God can do those things He sure *is* great."

Tim had experienced a moment of personal discovery. In the pattern for life-changing learning we refer to this as the *eureka!* — the moment when "the light goes on" and the student says, "Ah-ha, now I see." Because it is a personal affair, this discovery can occur at any time in the session and will vary from child to child. But through the planned learning activities and faithful prayer for each student, you can set the stage for important discoveries to be made.

The closing moments of the session should focus on how the children can put into practice — *enact* — the main ideas that have been talked about during the morning. Activities are sometimes suggested which allow the children to play out the real-life application in order to help them bridge the gap between the Sunday school classroom and the ordinary weekday setting. Activity sheets may be designed as home reminders of what the child can do.

Church Time

Sunday school was over, and the juniors, teens, and adults were making their way to the sanctuary. A hum of happy voices came from the nursery, kindergarten, and primary departments. Under the supervision of their teachers, children went to the rest rooms and made a stop at the drinking fountain.

Back inside the department room the teachers had prepared a game for the primary children. Soon they will be busily hunting for word cards hidden around the room. When the cards are found, the children will have the fun of seeing how much they can remember from the stories they have been hearing in Sunday school.

Since children have probably been sitting for some time in their Sunday school classes, it will be important to begin the church hour with activities which allow the boys and girls to become physically active. A time of review, games, story drama, and other activities will allow them to prepare for their worship time.

Especially with younger children, it is preferable to have one or two teachers work with the boys and girls for the total period Sunday morning. If the staff is rotated, this arrangement can be made without continually depriving teachers of both adult Sunday school classes and worship services. The following system might be used.

	September				October				November			
	Nursery SS	Nursery Church	Adult SS	Adult Church	Nursery SS	Nursery Church	Adult SS	Adult Church	Nursery SS	Nursery Church	Adult SS	Adult Church
Teacher A	X	X					X	X	X	X		
Teacher B	X	X			X	X					X	X
Teacher C			X	X	X	X			X	X		

The transition from Sunday school to church time should run smoothly. Church hour workers will need to be present and ready to begin working with the children as soon as Sunday school is dismissed. A smooth transition will call for cooperative planning on the part of the Sunday school and church hour staffs.

Organizing the Sunday School

Facilities, personnel, and the size of the Sunday school dictate how children are grouped in classes and departments. Although there are many variations on the theme, there are ideals concerning age level divisions that ought to be carefully considered.

Curriculum materials for each age level have been prepared with children of that particular age in mind. Therefore, curriculum pieces are most effective when they are used with the specific group for which they were designed. The following chart shows the various groupings which are desirable so that no child is required to use materials which are not designed for his or her age.

POSSIBLE GROUPINGS

Curriculum	Individual classes	Combined	Broadest grouping
Use nursery curriculum for 2- and 3-year-olds	2-year-old class(es) · 3-year-old class(es)	2-year-old·3-year-old class	2-and-3-year old class
Use kindergarten curriculum for 4- and 5-year-olds	4-year-old class(es) · 5-year-old class(es)	4- and 5-year old class	4-and-5-year class
Use primary curriculum for grades 1, 2, 3	1st grade class(es) · 2nd grade class(es) · 3rd grade class(es)	1st grade class; 2nd and 3rd grade class	1st, 2nd, and 3rd grade class
Use junior curriculum for grades 4, 5, 6	4th grade class(es) · 5th grade class(es) · 6th grade class(es)	4th grade class; 4th and 5th grade class; 5th and 6th grade class; 6th grade class	4th, 5th, and 6th grade class

Proper grouping of children is also important because of the curriculum cycle. Nursery and kindergarten materials are designed on a two-year cycle, primary and junior on a three-year cycle. The content of the Sunday school sessions repeats every two or three years. If classes are made up of combinations of ages or grades within the heavy lines on the above chart the children will never repeat materials. They will have moved on into the next department by the time the cycle begins again. But if the children in one class come from two age or grade level groups there is a problem. An example of this would be a class of third and fourth graders. The third graders should be using primary materials; the fourth graders, junior. If the class uses primary material, this means that the fourth graders will be studying the same lessons which they had in first grade, because the curriculum cycle is repeating. They will also be missing a whole year of junior studies.

In the chart you will notice that we have made only one suggestion for grouping primary children into two classes. Because the first graders are just learning to read, in most cases it is best to let them have their own class where they can have extra help from the teacher.

Within department divisions, group the children according to their needs. This may call for variations from year to year. In the Sunday school which has enough juniors for two classes some years the fourth graders may need their own class where they can have extra help from the teacher. Other times the sixth graders may be advanced and will need their own class with extra challenge to keep them interested. Another department may have an even number of boys and girls in fourth grade but only one girl in the fifth grade and only one boy in the sixth grade. The children in that department would probably be happiest with a fourth grade class, a fifth and sixth grade girls' class and a fifth and sixth grade boys' class.

The goal of Sunday school is to meet needs. Even traditional organizational structures should be evaluated regularly in the light of student needs.

Would You
1. explain how presession activities could benefit the Sunday school department in which you work?
2. match the following materials with the correct age or grade group?

Aldersgate Nursery Curriculum _____	a. grades 6 and 7
Aldersgate Kindergarten Curriculum _____	b. grades 1, 2, 3
	c. ages 3, 4, 5
Aldersgate Primary Curriculum _____	d. ages 2 and 3
	e. grades 4, 5, 6
Aldersgate Junior Curriculum _____	f. grades 3 and 4
	g. ages 4 and 5

Your Move
1. Take time right now to think about your classroom. What does it look like? What sort of impression are the children getting as they come? What can you do to improve the appearance of your classroom and assembly area?
2. Meet with the other workers in your department to talk about the use of time on Sunday morning. Is there adequate time for class activities? Does there need to be an adjustment in the length of the worship or assembly time? Can valuable minutes be added through presession activities?

6 Sunday School – A Part of the Whole

Can You
1. define the purpose of Sunday school?
2. list four advantages of team planning involving all who work with children in the church?

After studying chapter 6 you can.

Mark's eyes sparkle with mischief and life. It's his turn to practice his part for the Christmas program. "Here I am, you lucky people," he begins. The laughter of the other children obviously pleases him.

Jonathan is a handsome, intelligent child. But on Sunday morning he seems to be part of many little scuffles. With a twinkle in his eye he bumps another child, and good-naturedly the pushing and shoving begin. Is Jonathan a bad boy, or might he be starved for a little roughhousing and physical contact? You see, at home, he has only a baby sister, with whom he wouldn't dare to wrestle.

Sandra looks troubled. She is a serious, sensitive child, sometimes moody. When she is out of sorts, she refuses to cooperate. As the middle child in the family, she has not received as much attention as the other children have. Her parents have just begun to realize this.

Kevin is quiet. Sometimes the other children tease him. His parents are divorced, and his mother is planning to remarry. He will have to adjust to having a younger stepsister share his mother's affection.

Terry is a newcomer, a sweet cooperative child who never creates any problems in the Sunday school class. Her parents are just beginning to get acquainted with the church.

How much do you know about the boys and girls in your class? Do you know enough to meet needs?

The Focus of Our Ministry

What is the purpose of Sunday school and other Christian education programs in the church? Is our purpose to get through lessons, keep kids under control, and run a good program which is highly rated on someone's evaluation scale? Or do we work with boys and girls because we want to meet their needs? Everyone reading this book would certainly choose the latter purpose, but is our behavior as teachers always in line with the purpose of meeting the children's needs?

In the rush of living, it is easy to find time only to study our teacher's manual and not to get acquainted with our children, their needs and their interests. Knowing one's students takes listening, caring, and time: listening as the children visit during presession, really listening when they try to tell you something, caring enough to ask about the big event the child was anticipating last week, taking the time for informal activities outside of class, visiting in the home, or spending an evening at a grade school Christmas concert.

Effective teachers are not trucks loaded with biblical facts and concepts to be dumped on the children. They are pastors, shepherds, gardeners: persons who understand the general characteristics of children and are constantly trying to more adequately understand the individual children in their classes. Their concern is to have a part in meeting the needs of each child, bringing young lives into touch with God's love and truth.

Materials and programs were made to be fitted to children. Aldersgate session plans were not designed to be "gotten through." They were designed to be adapted to meet the needs of boys and girls. Sunday school, midweek programs, and other activities that are available for children in your church were designed with the needs of children in mind. But they will need additional adaptation to make them fit the needs of the particular children in those programs this year. The focus of our ministry must be on meeting the needs of boys and girls, not simply on going through the routine of teaching lessons and running programs.

It Can't All Be Done on Sunday Morning

In Colossians 1:28 (RSV), Paul states the purpose of his ministry; to "... present every man mature in Christ." Christian maturity does not apply to some spiritual dimension of man which can be separated out from everything else that he is. Social, emotional, intellectual, spiritual maturity are all wrapped up in the phrase "mature in Christ." For the grace of God is applicable to every area of personality. Teachers need to be concerned about the total person.

Maturing in Christ is a lifelong process which takes seven days a week. The experiences of Sunday school can have an influence on this maturing process, but they make up only one small segment of the person's learning experiences. Persons are constantly learning. At school, at home, and through everything that happens at church, the child is learning and constructing his understanding of the world, of God, and of his relationships with others. The atmosphere of the church will have a profound influence upon the child.

A Place to Learn and Grow

The community which is healthy for moral and spiritual growth is a community characterized by warmth, acceptance, love, respect, and openness. Words gain their meaning from personal experiences. For a child to understand what the teacher means when he talks about love, that child must have experienced the kind of love the teacher is referring to. How can Johnny comprehend the fact that God accepts him and loves him when no one else does, if he has not experienced acceptance from others?

Questions and doubts may destroy faith, or they may be the prelude to significant growth. The atmosphere of the church and the home may make the difference. If children or young people attend a church where there is openness, they can ask questions and find caring adults who will work through those questions and doubts with them, helping them to gain exciting new understandings.

For a Sunday school to have long-range effectiveness it needs to be part of a church which genuinely cares about its boys and girls. Let the rest of the church know about the children's departments in your Sunday school. You might invite adult classes to visit the children's departments and observe what goes on during Sunday school. Let the children share some of the songs and Scripture passages they are learning as a part of the adult worship service. Encourage adults to get acquainted with the boys and girls and greet them warmly by name whenever they see them at church or in the community. Enlist adults who are not Sunday school teachers as prayer partners and share with them prayer concerns from time to time.

The church can provide important social ties and experiences for children. Especially during the late junior and teen years the peer group will greatly influence the child or young person. The importance of church friends may make the difference between a young person going God's way or going the way of the world. During the years of childhood we can help the boys and girls develop strong friendships with one another. The midweek clubs and activities of the church and social functions related with Sunday school provide the opportunity for these bonds to be established. Care should be taken that the fellowship of the church group not become exclusive. It should provide the children with a nucleus of good friends and a source of enjoyable experiences in which they will want to include other friends from school and the community.

A Coordinated Ministry

When we consider what there is to be learned about God's work through history, who He is, what redemption means, and what He wants to do in our lives, we become overwhelmed with the task of introducing boys and girls to all of the exciting things there are to learn. One hour on Sunday morning does not provide adequate time to do all that is needed to help boys and girls mature in Christ. The worship hour for the children each Sunday morning is an important part of their experience. Weekday clubs, children's choirs, vacation Bible school, camping experiences — all of these are important parts of the total ministry of Christian education, the ministry of meeting the needs of children.

Each organization or program in the church should have as its focus the meeting of the needs of those involved in the program. Some needs, such as the need for love, acceptance, and respect must be met through all activities; but no program fully meets all needs. We must design our operations so that each program complements the others.

Sunday school has a special contribution to make to the child. The Sunday school is viewed as the Bible study hour of the week. This is the time when we endeavor to systematically help the child lay a firm foundation of biblical understandings upon which he or she can build a healthy Christian life. We want to lead the children in an exploration of God's Word. During the Sunday school period, we endeavor to help them build their understanding of God and their relationship with Him. We help them discover the guidelines which He gives for living and how these can be applied to the specific experiences of childhood. The Sunday school provides the baseline of biblical and theological content, both of which must be applied to the individual's life if they are to have meaning.

Other programs supplement the Sunday school. They provide learning activities which are difficult or impossible to fit into the Sunday school program. Midweek clubs, VBS, choirs, and camps give opportunity for other needed experiences and the exploration of other important content.

To do the best possible job of ministering to the needs of boys and girls, all persons involved in the local church Christian education program will need to be working together as a team, coordinating their ministries. It is important for each worker to understand the special focus and purpose of the various Christian education organizations. Teamwork calls for planning together regularly. Those persons who work with children should meet together each quarter. This includes those involved in the Sunday school, weekday clubs, children's church, choirs, VBS, and any other ministry to children. The following list identifies a few of the advantages of teamwork and cooperative planning.

1. Sharing with others who work with the same children as we do will often uncover new understandings and insights that we need.

2. We gain encouragement from one another as we plan together. It is much easier to get discouraged when we feel we are working all alone. Just to know that another teacher is having similar difficulties encourages us to trust God for needed help. Knowing what God is doing in another setting rekindles our faith.

3. There is a special dynamic in praying with others for special concerns. As children's workers pray together for the boys and girls they minister to, they will find a new effectiveness in their ministry.

4. As we discover the purpose and emphasis of other organizations or ministries we have a

better understanding of where to place our priorities in the use of the limited amount of time which we have with the boys and girls.

5. As workers study the needs of children and look at what is being offered through the various programs, together they can identify the needs which are not being met.

6. A sharing of ideas among workers will be helpful in coming up with the best adaptations of programs for the meeting of needs.

Working with the Home

The ministry of the church in the life of the child is important. But, God has given first responsibility for religious instruction to parents. In Deuteronomy 6:7 Moses commanded parents to teach God's commands diligently to their children as they lived with them through common, everyday events. One of the major responsibilities of the church is to help parents fulfill their responsibilities under God. As teachers of children we can have a ministry to their homes.

We say, "Our church cares about you and your family." The Sunday school teacher demonstrates the truth of this statement as he calls to say how much he appreciates having Kevin in the class or to ask whether Tammy is sick.

Make regular contact with the home a part of your ministry to children. Shortly after a child joins your class, visit the home and share with the parents the materials which will be used in

Sunday school. Explain the story papers, activity sheets, or Bible study guides the children will be bringing home from week to week. Introduce parents to *Table Talk.*

A camera might be a helpful tool for making additional contacts with the home. Make a practice of taking candid shots of your boys and girls during presession or when you are out on informal activities together. When these have been developed, take the class album to the home and show it to the children and their parents. You may even want to have extra prints made of some of the shots so that you can give one to each family.

As teachers in the children's department of the Sunday school we can invite parents to Sunday school. This invitation will be strengthened immensely if it is followed up by a visit from an adult Sunday school teacher and a couple from the class which the parents might attend. Provide adult teachers with the names of your children's parents. In our rapidly changing mobile society, people are longing for the warmth of a group to which they can belong. The church is to be a center of God's love. Being a part of the church will become attractive when we carry the warmth of God's genuine love to homes and open our fellowship to families.

Pray for the families of your students. Children's needs will most likely be met when they have Christian homes and a church that loves and cares for them. God intended that the church and the home should work together to help boys and girls mature in Christ.

Would You
1. define the purpose of Sunday school?
2. list four advantages of team planning involving all who work with children?

Your Move
1. Plan an informal activity for your class within the next two weeks.
2. Ask a couple from an adult Sunday school class to visit the homes of any of your children whose parents do not come to church.

Leader's Guide

Introduction

As leader of this training course you are a model teacher. Persons tend to teach as they are taught. It will be easier for the members of your class to apply the ideas presented in this book if they see them in action as you lead their time of group study. Plan each session to incorporate the steps of life-changing learning.

Throughout each session the learners should be actively involved in the learning process. Begin each class period with an activity to *engage* the minds of the learners — something that will pull each person into participation. *Exploration* of new ideas is to be done mainly through the reading of the text. For each session ask various learners to say what they thought were the most important ideas in the chapter studied for the current session. This will bring the ideas into focus and prepare the way for discussing any questions which grow out of the reading.

Most of the group session time will be spent *examining* your Sunday school and discovering how the ideas of the text can be applied in each class and department, by each teacher.

Encourage the learners to act upon what they are learning — *enact*. Each week give opportunity for reporting on action taken as suggested in "Your Move." Some of the learning activities in the following session plans will allow the learners to act on new ideas in the group session.

Curriculum samples will be needed for several learning activities. Have teachers bring their Aldersgate curriculum materials to class each week. If your Sunday school is not currently using Aldersgate materials, order samples from your publishing house.

The filmstrip *AGC Is Great!* is suggested for use in session two. It may be available from the board of Christian education in your conference or area. If not, you may order it from your publishing house.

Give reading assignments for each session. If possible, have the learners read chapter 1 before the first session. If this is impossible have the first two chapters read before the second session. The reading material should be studied individually before the session in which it is to be discussed. Throughout the course encourage the participants to keep up on their reading. This will make the group study more interesting and profitable for them.

In the following pages you will find some ideas which can be used in the group study times. Supplement these with your own ideas and lead your group in an exciting time of life-changing learning.

Here are three activities designed to help you lead your students to a clearer, more personal understanding of some of the content of this chapter.

Activity I. Bible study to discover Jesus' teaching methods. Each student should have a notebook, Bible, and pen.

A. John 8:6-8. Jesus used a method here which often works with children. First, He did something to divert the attention of His hearers. What was it? Next, He gave instructions to them. What were His instructions? Last, He gave them an opportunity to change their behavior without apparently having to be observed by their teacher. What did He do? What behavior change took place?

B. Make copies of the following instructions and chart for use by the learners during the class session. Listed below in column 1 are other methods and/or techniques Jesus used. In column 2 are Scripture references. Match them. Then discuss when, how, and with what age group you can effectively use each of these:

(a) answer question with question
(b) used idiom and culture of time
(c) taught in the church (lecture)
(d) used an axiom to answer question
(e) personal touch
(f) acknowledged His own need to meet the need of another
(g) object lesson
(h) story telling
(i) dialogue

(1) Mark 12:13-17
(2) Matthew 9:12
(3) Matthew 9:29
(4) John 18:33-38
(5) John 6:11
(6) John 4:6-7
(7) Matthew 12:10-13
(8) Mark 12:1-13
(9) Matthew 13:54

Activity II. Curriculum Search. Each student will need a teacher's manual, and pen or pencil. Working independently, or in groups, look for examples in the teacher's manual of methods and/or techniques, similar to those Jesus used. Note where these are found. Discuss with entire group similarities you discover.

Activity III. Cycle Chart Study. In the back of the teacher's manual is a cycle chart for the age level and a spiral diagram of all age levels for the current quarter of AGC. Compare the study for various age levels during the quarter covered.

If additional time is available, divide into groups.

Discuss:

1. Role of the teacher in establishing rapport with children.
2. Ways the teacher may express feelings of warmth and love to boys and girl.

Share the findings with larger group.

Activity: Show the filmstrip *AGC Is Great* and then use the following questions and activities (If the filmstrip is not available, the questions and activities may be used separately.) Distribute teachers' manuals to entire group (or ask them to bring their own with them).

A. Lead the teachers to identify in their own manuals the five elements or steps in life-changing learning. Begin by having the group help you list them on the chalkboard. Lead them in discussing each of the steps to be sure everyone understands the kind of activity being referred to:

1. Engage: Activities with which the session begins — attention getters. Something to touch the interest of the students and lead them into the exploration of the session.

2. Explore: Techniques to involve students in thinking through concepts and ideas from the Scriptures.

3. Eureka: Insights the teacher hopes students will discover. (May be identified from objectives of session.)

4. Examine: Techniques to help students look at their own lives, and try to apply the new insights to situations they face.

5. Enact: Activities planned to help students live out, during the coming week, the emphases from the session.

B. Divide into groups according to age levels. Give each group a sheet of paper. On the left side of the sheet, in a column, list the five steps: engage, explore, eureka, examine, and enact. In groups, they will read through the "Class Time" section of next Sunday's Session. Under each of the five headings, the group should list activities/tools they will use to help the students take that particular step in discovery learning. Perhaps the following questions will help:

1. What will you do to *engage* the minds of your students, to grasp their attention, to prepare them for learning?

2. What activities will be used to help the students *explore* God's Word and the concepts of this session?

3. What discovery do you hope to help your students make during the session?

4. What will you do to help the students *examine* their own life situations in the light of what they are learning?

5. What will you plan to help the students *enact* (or put into practice) what they have learned?

C. As time permits, groups may share with each other from the outlines they have just completed.

As the class members arrive give each of them two three-by-five-inch cards. To begin the session ask them to write on the first card one thing they remember from reading chapter 3. Take a few minutes for sharing what was written on the cards. This will provide a recap of the chapter.

Divide the class into department groups — nursery, kindergarten, primary, and junior. Have each group look over the various Aldersgate curriculum pieces for their age level. Here are some directions to help them get started. It would be good to provide copies of these instructions for each group.

Teachers' manuals: Note the different units of study — titles, number of weeks in each; find ideas for presession time; find and underline three pupil-involvement ideas. What makes these ideas appropriate for this age child?

Pupil books or activity sheets: What kinds of variety do you find? Locate an activity designed to review the Bible story. Find an activity designed to reinforce the life application. Share any insights discovered while working through the "Your Move" section of chapter 3.

Teaching resources: Find the items that can be manipulated by the pupils. What different kinds of visuals are in the packet? Which items are reinforcement for the Bible story?

If your class members have already been using the Aldersgate curriculum, they can share together what they have found especially helpful and ask questions as to how others are using the various pieces.

If your group is small, this curriculum study may be done individually or in pairs.

Allow time for the groups to show their curriculum pieces to the whole class. Suggest that they quickly display the individual pieces from the resource packets. Seeing these all out at once almost always produces a very striking effect among teachers.

Next talk about the importance of a strong link between the home and the Sunday school. Ask the teachers, "Which items in your age level package will link the home and Sunday school together?" Give time for each group to show its items. Talk together about ways that this tie can be strengthened in your Christian education program. Help teachers think creatively about beginning (or continuing) an active program of contacting parents and children in their homes. Also, you might help primary and junior teachers think of ways for getting better acquainted with their classes through special activities such as having parties, making cookies together, or going fishing. Time spent with a child away from Sunday school is the best way of showing the child that the teacher really loves him. Preschool teachers can plan get-acquainted activities for the pupils and their families. Potluck dinners or picnics are good starters.

For the closing moments of this session have everyone turn to I Samuel 12:23. If there are not enough Bibles on hand, have the verse written on a chalkboard for everyone to see. Have a time of quietness when each teacher will think about the individual students in his or her care. Then, have them write this verse on the second card they were given at the first of the session. Encourage the class members to take the card home and use it to remind them to pray for the boys and girls of the church. Close with prayer.

Ahead of time ask two people to debate the topic "Prepared: To Be or Not to Be!" One person will speak for two minutes on the importance of good study habits and thorough preparation even for busy people with many other responsibilities. The other speaker will defend the fact that he doesn't have much time to prepare, so he will just have to rely on the Holy Spirit to lead him on Sunday morning instead of making many plans ahead that might even constrict the working of the Lord.

Session Four
Be Prepared

Begin the session with the debate on the subject of preparation. After the speakers have finished, open the meeting for discussion from the group. Perhaps some will wish to share personal experiences of times when good preparation saved the day or even of times when non-prepared sessions turned into disasters.

If the following points are not mentioned some time during the discussion, you may bring them up for emphasis:

1. Aldersgate writers and editors seek the guidance of God as they prepare the materials far in advance. Teachers have told them about specific times when the Holy Spirit blessed a class session in a special way or ministered to the teacher through a part of the lesson. This is direct evidence of God's ability to lead in advance.

2. God does things in an orderly, organized fashion. He is pleased to work with us within this sort of framework. Preparing ahead of time does not limit God's ability to work with us and our students. Many times changes have to be made in plans, but God is faithful to help make those adjustments when we have prepared and done our part ahead of time.

Suggest that the group share their concerns about session preparation. Ask: What makes it difficult for you to prepare adequately? Discuss the problem of limited time for preparation. Finding time for organized study, being self-disciplined enough to stick with a regular schedule, and putting out effort for preparing visuals are common problems. Suggest that each one write out his or her own individual time schedule for preparation. Have the teachers share their plans. Refer to the suggested study scheduled on page 57. Help them to know that beginning early in the week is important. Urge a new commitment for regular study habits, beginning now.

93

Divide the class into department groups — nursery, kindergarten, primary, junior. Assign one person in each group to act as leader. This could be done in advance. Have the groups conduct a partial pre-quarter planning session. Ideas for this kind of meeting are on page 56. Have each group pray about two concerns in their department and then scan the titles and goals of the session plans for the next four Sundays. Assign each group one or two questions from page 56 to discuss. Give opportunity for each group to tell about one discovery or plan that came out of this planning session.

If you have department leaders present, you might close by having each department set the date for their next planning session.

Session Five
On Sunday Morning

Begin by having two people role-play the following situations. They will do it in monologue form, pretending to be receiving response from a group of children.

1. Teacher sits down, spreads his material out, and says to the class, "Okay, quiet down now. We've got a lesson to get through this morning." (He can then ad-lib the situation, imagining that pupils will not be quiet or pay attention as he tries to start the Bible story.)

2. Teacher comes in and immediately begins this activity (actual example from a copy of Fall *Kindergarten Teacher*):

Show the children a surprise bag. In it you should have a coat which is too small for even your smallest child. Let the children guess what you have in the bag. Then pull out the coat and invite one of your larger pupils to try it on. Then tell the following story: "A New Coat for Samuel." (The role player can ad-lib the situation of the children becoming happily involved. Cut the role playing just as the teacher begins the Bible story.)

Discuss with the group the results that each teacher likely had. Throw out a thought question: "Which teacher are you most like?"

Teachers may then take a look at their manuals, noticing the suggestions for how to prepare the way for the Bible story in next Sunday's session.

Review the term *discovery learning*. Help the class members to understand what it means. Learning cannot be poured into children's minds through their ears. The student must be actively involved in discovering not only the facts but also what those facts can mean to his personal life. The teacher provides activities through which important discoveries can be made. It is as the child becomes actively involved in these learning experiences that learning takes place. This is discovery learning.

Divide into departmental groups. Give each group a large strip of shelf paper and a marking pen. Have the groups go through at least two sessions in the teacher's manual for their departments (a whole unit if time permits). On the large strips of paper have them list all the activities suggested in the teacher's manual which actually involve the children (examples: music, conversation, directed play, creative art, story play, verse or story review).

The groups may name briefly some of the student activities which they discovered.

Have each group plan one, or preferably two, presession activities to offer next Sunday. Group members should divide the responsibilities for preparing and conducting the presession activities.

Another question to discuss would be: Are changes needed in facilities or organization of classes and scheduling to allow for greater student involvement? If this question is discussed, encourage the groups to come up with concrete suggestions for change.

Divide the group into three departmental sections. Provide each section with a marking pen and one strip of the paper labeled for the appropriate age level — nursery, kindergarten, primary, or junior. For five to ten minutes each section will think of and write down on the paper characteristics and needs of the age level designated on their paper.

Session Six
Sunday School — a Part of the Whole

Have each section share the characteristics and needs which they wrote down. Add any that you have thought of that they did not include.

Talk about how each pupil is an individual. Not all children fit into a certain mold; their needs vary. Teachers should remember that they are not teaching a class — they are teaching a group of *individuals.*

Lead the group in discussing the following questions:

Are we adequately meeting the needs of our boys and girls?

What more can we do to meet needs?

What can we do to increase our ministry to the homes of our boys and girls?

As a summary exercise for this course have the teachers prepare a lesson plan for next Sunday's session. Provide them with worksheets similar to the one pictured below on which to write the lesson plan. This will help them follow the pattern for life-changing learning. Ideas for specific learning activities will be found in their Aldersgate teacher's manual.

SESSION PLANNING SHEET

Session Title _____

Session Focus _____

Session Goal (revised as needed) _____

_____

Teaching Methods — Activities

ENGAGE (involve, interest, captivate attention)	
EXPLORE (investigate, study, gather information)	
EUREKA (the joy of discovery)	
EXAMINE (infer, generalize, draw conclusions)	
ENACT (implement plan or take action)	

Close the session with a reminder as to the purpose of curriculum, the reasons for session preparation, for taking time to attractively arrange the classroom, for spending time with pupils in order to get to know them and be better able to meet their needs, for taking time for the teaching task itself — life-changing learning. When teachers are careful to do their best in every way, God takes what is offered and multiplies it into life-changing results. A teacher may not see those results during the time a child is in his class, but he can trust God. When the gospel is faithfully presented in ways that attract and interest a child so that he can understand what is being said, it will not return void. God has promised it will accomplish its purpose. Isaiah 55:11.